A Creative Minds Biography

TALES FOR HARD TIMES

A Story about Charles Dickens

by David R. Collins

illustrations by David Mataya

M Millbrook Press/Minneapolis

To editor Marybeth Lorbiecki

Millbrook Press, Inc.
A division of Lerner Publishing Group
241 First Avenue North
Minneapolis, MN 55401 U.S.A.

Website address: www.lernerbooks.com

Library of Congress Cataloging-in-Publication Data

Collins, David R.
    Tales for hard times ; a story about Charles Dickens /
by David R. Collins : illustrated by David Mataya.
        p.   cm. — (A creative minds book)
    Includes bibliographical references.
    Summary: Follows the life and works of the popular nineteenth-century
English author.
    ISBN-13: 978-0-87614-433-6 (lib. bdg. : alk. paper)
    ISBN-10: 0-87614-433-4 (lib. bdg. : alk. paper)
    1. Dickens, Charles, 1812–1870—Biography—Juvenile literature. 2. Novel-
ists, English—19th century—Biography—Juvenile literature. [1. Dickens,
Charles, 1812–1870. 2. Authors, English.] I. Mataya, David, ill.
II. Title. III. Series.
PR4581.C66   1990
823'.8—dc20
[B]   90-32490
[92]

Manufactured in the United States of America
3 4 5 6 7 8 – MA – 11 10 09 08 07 06

TALES FOR HARD TIMES

Table of Contents

① A Lively British Lad

No one in the entire British Empire could tell stories like Mary Weller. Eight-year-old Charles Dickens was sure of that! Every night Charles would sit before the young family maid as she told her strange tales in the attic nursery.

The four other Dickens children might head sleepily off to their beds, but not Charles. He did not want to miss a single word. He could see the wild stallion with its tongue of fire, roaming the countryside and torching the hair off schoolboys' heads. And then there was the dreadful Captain Murderer, who slaughtered his wives and baked them in pies. Scary? Indeed! Exciting? Always. Mary Weller could make even the boldest and bravest lad shiver under his covers.

John Dickens, Charles's father, could tell a fine story himself. But instead of the simple language of Mary Weller, Master Dickens preferred elaborate words, with syllables running over syllables.

The son of a housekeeper and a butler, John always wanted to be something more than a servant. By 1820 he had worked as a clerk for the Navy Pay Office for fifteen years. Yet his salary was not large, and he often spent more than a few shillings entertaining relatives and friends. Elizabeth Dickens, his wife, shared the hosting honors. Even when there were no guests, Elizabeth served large meals and dressed in the latest fashions.

With such extravagances, John Dickens's salary seldom stretched to the end of the month. Many times instead of payments, bill collectors received apologies and promises.

But bills or no bills, the Dickenses put time, energy, and eventually money into the education of their children. Born February 7, 1812, Charles had begun his schooling at home at an early age. His mother had sparked his interest in reading and writing, and had started him off on a little Latin as well. As Elizabeth taught and read stories to all her eager children—first Fanny and Charles, and then Letitia, Harriet, and Fred—she would act out scenes with funny faces and voices.

Stories came to life even more vividly for Charles when they were performed on the stages of local playhouses. John and Elizabeth loved going to the theater, and they took their children with them at every opportunity. Charles—a small, slight child—would strain forward in his seat to catch every word and gesture.

Yet Charles didn't need a playhouse to enjoy the theater. Mounting the kitchen table, he had his own stage. He would act out parts of the plays he had seen or ones he had made up himself. No one would see an undersized boy of eight with pale skin and long curls. Why, Charles could give a performance good enough for King George himself!

The talents of Charles Dickens and his sister Fanny (who had a beautiful voice and could act as well) were no secret in the village of Chatham, England. John and Elizabeth sometimes brought their children down to the local Mitre Inn. While customers sipped their ale and nibbled on tarts, Charles and Fanny performed songs, poems, and scenes from plays.

That Charlie will make you proud, more than one guest told the smiling parents.

He was born for the stage, another observed.

True enough, John Dickens agreed. A life in the theater, though, demanded both talent and strength. Charles appeared healthy and sturdy while performing, but he often suffered from seizures that left him in a crumpled heap. "Colic" the doctors called it. Charles seldom lasted through a fast game of cricket or prisoner's base.

By the time Charles was eight, he and Fanny were attending a neighborhood dame school. Free public schools did not exist then. So the Dickenses paid an educated woman to teach their children in her home.

The rooms of the schoolmistress were located above a small shop. A little pug-nosed dog stood guard in the building's second-floor hallway. Charles felt the dog's hot breath on his ankles more than once as he and Fanny made a dash for their teacher's door.

The distractions in the schoolmistress's home were many, yet Charles proved an able student. Even so, when the Dickenses moved in 1821, Charles's education improved considerably. His new neighborhood in Chatham boasted a *real* classroom. The schoolmaster, William Giles, was a recent graduate of Oxford University.

Charles quickly became a proud member of "Giles's Cats." He and the other schoolboys wore white beaver hats and teased students from nearby schools. They organized games in local hay fields, rowed boats on the Medway River, and skated in winter. Charles grew stronger with all the exercise.

The move, however, was a step down for the Dickens family. The new house cost less to rent (which is why the family moved), but it hardly compared with the three-story brick house the Dickenses had left behind.

Yet "The Brook," as people called the Dickenses' new home, was a secure place for Charles. In a tiny hideaway next to the attic nursery, the boy spent many a lazy afternoon reading the novels his father had stored there.

Shortly after the family's move to The Brook, a stepcousin of the children, named James Lamert, Jr., came to live with the Dickenses. One of the sixteen-year-old youth's favorite pastimes was going to the theater. He often invited Charles to accompany him to the playhouse in the city of Rochester, which was three miles away. On the stage, swords glittered in the candlelight, songs filled the air, a clown juggled, a queen fell dead. Such magic and mystery!

Outside the theater's walls, Rochester bustled with activity. Charles and his father often walked to the city from their house in Chatham.

One day John Dickens kept walking as he passed Rochester's High Street, journeying into the country fields beyond. Charles hurried to keep up with his father's long strides. Finally John stopped.

"Look over there, at that hilltop," he said, pointing.

Charles gazed as ordered. On the hill sat a great brick house with handsome bowed windows and fine white columns. Ivy vines climbed the home's stone walls. Gad's Hill Place was its name.

"Someday, lad," Master Dickens declared, "you may live in such a place if you work hard and find success. Why, you may live in that very house for all we know."

Charles's eyes widened. Gad's Hill. Could a person like himself ever live in such a place?

Charles and his father went back to Gad's Hill again and again. The beautiful home on the hilltop became part of a dream for Charles. But in the path of fulfilling that dream lurked a nightmare—a nightmare more frightening to Charles than any of Mary Weller's terrifying tales.

②
Daytime Nightmares

In March 1822, another baby was born to the Dickens family. Expenses piled up.

That autumn the Navy Pay Office transferred John Dickens to London. The family said good-bye to Mary Weller. Furniture was sold rather than moved, and what little was left, the Dickenses packed up for their new London home. Charles stayed behind in Chatham with Master Giles to finish the school term.

When Christmas came, Charles's time as one of Giles's Cats came to an end. Master Giles, sorry to see this talented pupil leaving, presented Charles with a gift—a slim book by Oliver Goldsmith called *The Bee*.

Thoroughly downcast, the silent ten-year-old boy boarded a coach for London. A cold drizzle fell.

He sat alone and ate a sandwich, and the smell of wet straw filled his nostrils. As the horses's hooves clattered on the cobblestone streets, Charles watched the places he loved fade from view. Life suddenly seemed sadder and more confusing to him than he had ever expected it to be.

In the Camden Town area of London, the Dickenses lived elbow to elbow. When Charles arrived, he thought he would be able to go to school in his new surroundings. But there were too many mouths to feed and too little money.

Instead, Charles had to clean his father's boots, look after the younger children, and serve as an errand boy. His old illnesses returned—the attacks and fever.

In April 1823, Fanny received a music scholarship. Off she went to study and live at the Royal Academy of Music in London. Charles would have given anything he owned to follow her—to go to a school to learn about something, somewhere.

As family debts grew, tempers flared. Elizabeth declared that she was going to open a dame school. She went out and rented a grand house on Gower Street that she figured could serve as a school as well as a home. The Dickens family moved again.

But nobody ever came to the new school. No one even inquired about it. One by one, household items were sold to local shops. Charles even had to cart away the novels he so dearly loved.

James Lamert, Charles's theater-going cousin, soon took his leave too. But James returned for a visit, and when he did, he brought news. He had found work for Charles at Warren's Blacking—the boot-polish factory he managed.

Charles hated the idea. But the job paid six shillings a week, and his parents were grateful for any extra money. In addition, James promised the Dickenses that he would give Charles school lessons during dinner breaks.

Thus it was settled. On a Monday morning in February 1824, two days after his twelfth birthday, Charles went off to his first day of work.

The dirty, tumbledown warehouse of Warren's Blacking sat at the edge of the River Thames. Charles's workbench was placed in James's office, on the second floor. From eight o'clock in the morning to eight o'clock in the evening, Charles pasted oilpaper and then blue paper around small pots of boot polish. Afterward he clipped out labels and pasted them on the covered pots. As Charles worked, the squeaks of rats and the shouts of other boys drifted up to him from the story below.

Charles's lessons with his stepcousin quickly disappeared, as James became too busy. Charles was moved to the common workroom downstairs. He felt trapped and alone. The boys working with him were rough and had little or no schooling at all. They made fun of Charles, calling him a "young gentleman."

Charles's hopes of becoming an educated man seemed ruined. "No words can express the agony of my soul," Charles wrote later, "as I sunk into this companionship. . . ."

While Charles worked long, hard days, his father cowered at home. Master Dickens was afraid of being thrown into a debtors' prison for not paying his bills. Eleven days after Charles started working, constables banged on the Dickenses' door. John Dickens was arrested.

In the early morning fog, Charles walked with his father to the gates of Marshalsea Prison.

"The sun has set on me forever," John Dickens whispered to his son, moving wearily toward the prison's iron gates.

Charles watched his father with deep sorrow and shame. The boy felt his heart was going to break.

Soon after John Dickens's entry into Marshalsea Prison, the rest of the family moved in with him. This was not unusual. Debtors' families often chose to live with the debtors to avoid paying rent. Family members could come and go as they wished and use the prison's community kitchen to make meals.

Although John Dickens was not allowed to go to work, he still received some wages from the navy. He had been granted sick leave because of a kidney problem. With his sick pay, John could feed his wife and youngest children within the prison walls.

But Charles was left to fend for himself. His parents did not want him sleeping on the cold, damp prison floor. So they arranged for the boy to stay with an elderly friend in Camden Town.

Six days a week, Charles trudged over two and a half miles to the warehouse and then back. Every Saturday evening, Charles would collect his six-shilling wage and carefully wrap up each coin—one to spend for each day of the coming workweek. A shilling bought only something to drink and a single plate of beef and a biscuit; or a drink and a small platter of cheese and bread. Now and then Charles ate even less than this so he could splurge on a pudding or something to read. The adventure stories in the *Portfolio of Entertaining and Instructive Varieties of History, Literature and Fine Arts, etc.* sometimes proved too tempting to be resisted.

Charles saw his family only on Sundays. Each Sunday morning, Charles would wake early and hurry over to the Royal Academy to pick up Fanny. Together they would make their way to the prison.

Charles's time with his family passed quickly, too quickly. Then came six more days of pasting, cruel jeers, and an empty stomach. Charles had just an hour break for lunch and a half hour for midafternoon tea. Since he had little to eat, Charles would take long walks during his breaks. He would stare at food in the markets or watch other working children. They were dirty and hungry; their clothes were ragged. Some were bent over or crippled from work. Charles was one of them, and his body was suffering too. His fevered attacks had grown more frequent and severe.

None of the boys at Warren's Blacking knew about John Dickens's imprisonment. Charles guarded that secret. "I suffered exquisitely," he recalled later. "No one ever knew but I."

Fanny's progress at the Royal Academy plunged

Charles into deeper misery. If only *I* might have a chance . . . , a voice within him groaned.

A month had passed since his father's imprisonment. One Sunday evening, Charles broke down and sobbed to his father. The boy felt cast away, deserted. John took pity on his son, and a new place to live was found for Charles. It was closer to the prison and the warehouse. Now Charles could easily race to Marshalsea to have breakfast and dinner with his family.

It didn't matter to Charles that his new room was little more than a closet in an attic. A small window looked out over a timber yard, and when the tiny pane was opened, the fresh scent of cut wood floated in. The room was his and his alone, and Charles later wrote, "I thought it was paradise."

His new room, though, did not take Charles away from the blacking factory. He was hungry, and he was tired. On the streets, in the warehouse, and in the prison, Charles saw faces lined and leathered from years of too much work and too little pay. He smelled the garbage lining the streets and filling the gutters.

The faces, the sounds, and the smells would never be forgotten. Never.

③

With Pen in Hand

In May 1824, about a month after Charles moved, John Dickens stood before the Court of King's Bench and declared all his debts. He promised to pay them when he could. So the court released John from prison, and the Dickens family started their life anew.

Charles, however, remained a prisoner to his duties at Warren's Blacking for almost another year. The business moved to the busy area of Covent Garden. Charles and an older boy named Bob Fagin worked at benches near a large street window. Each day people stood gawking as the boys wrapped, pasted, and clipped; wrapped, pasted, and clipped.

One day in spring 1825, a familiar face appeared at the door. John Dickens watched his son for only a few minutes. Soon after, a letter was delivered to James Lamert. In it John criticized Lamert for treating Charles in such a dreadful manner.

An insulted Lamert sent the boy home.

Elizabeth Dickens tried hard to mend the quarrel, but her husband refused to budge. The boy would not go back.

Charles rejoiced at his father's decision, and he felt betrayed by his mother. He couldn't believe she wanted him to be sent back.

Several days later, John sent Charles to the Wellington House Academy on Hampstead Road to ask about the current rates for tuition. John had just been granted his retirement from the navy, and he had a small pension to spend.

Charles's nightmare was over! He was going back to school.

Wellington House Academy was a school for gentlemen, and it had a fine reputation. Dressed in a new dark jacket and trousers, Charles made his entrance. The short, curly-haired youth tried to appear older and better off than he was. He pledged that no one would know about his past.

In no time at all, Charles emerged as a class leader, both in studies and in mischief. He often carried the class mascot, a white mouse, squiggling and squirming under his shirt while his teachers droned on about numbers or Latin verbs.

Outside of class, penny magazines, with their

wild tales of terror, were passed from classmate to classmate. When no one had a pence to spend, Charles wrote such stories himself.

Your stories are better than those in the mags, more than one schoolmate noted.

It was only a short leap for Charles from the written page to the acting stage. He wrote plays for himself and his friends to perform. One dramatic production ended with a toy-theater set being blown up by firecrackers. This stupendous event brought the police pounding on the academy's door.

In the meantime, John Dickens had slid back into his poor spending habits. Bills mounted rapidly with the birth of Augustus in 1827. Only necessities could be afforded on John's small pension. After two years, Charles's days at the academy ended.

Now fifteen and quite educated for the son of a clerk, Charles did not return to the blacking warehouse. Surely the world had more to offer!

Charles worked for a short time as an office boy and then applied at the law firm of Ellis and Blackmore for a position as a clerk. With a blend of charm and enthusiasm, Charles got the job.

Still undersized and youthful, Charles again tried to look older, reporting for work in a blue jacket and military cap. He copied various legal documents and kept the accounting ledger. The young clerk thought clearly, wrote legibly, and had no trouble adding and subtracting figures. But he soon grew bored.

Through his work in the law office, Charles became familiar with the courts. In courtrooms known as Doctors' Commons, free-lance reporters were hired to take notes on cases being tried. The work paid well to reporters who could take notes quickly. Some court reporters eventually became note takers in the Parliamentary Press Gallery. Charles thought reporting was worth a try.

Charles's father was now working as a newspaper reporter. With his help, Charles learned shorthand—a quick method of taking notes with circles, dots, and dashes. Then he made his way to Doctors' Commons.

On giant wooden chairs, black- and red-robed judges sat, their wigs fashionably powdered gray. The chambers smelled musty and stale, and grim-faced lawyers filled the air with endless talk. Charles entered a rented reporter's box in the Consistory Court, surprising those in other boxes. At sixteen he was the youngest reporter ever to work at Doctors' Commons.

No one selected Charles the first day. Nor the

second. But on the third day, one of the court's directors asked him to record a case about a church will. Charles carefully noted every detail.

Word spread swiftly about the young journalist's quick and accurate reporting. Soon Charles was working every day.

Almost every evening, Charles went to the theater. Fanny and her friends often met him there or invited him to parties afterward. In 1829 Charles started to pay special attention to one of the young women in Fanny's group of friends. Maria Beadnell was a well-educated girl, "an angel in looks and manners" whose dark ringlets framed bright, snapping eyes. Charles fell in love.

For the next four years, Charles spent many hours at the Beadnell home. He courted Maria with long letters and little gifts. She delighted in his attention and sent him similar things through a friend.

On his eighteenth birthday (having reached the age requirement), Charles applied for a permit to read books at London's British Museum. This was one way he could continue his education. As often as he could, he would climb the stairs to the second floor of the museum and join the silent figures poring over books and manuscripts.

Shakespeare, Jonson, Goldsmith, Smollett, and Fielding—Charles read them all and many others. One thing was certain. Charles did not intend to be a court reporter all his life.

Wanting to impress Maria and her family, Charles started taking acting lessons at a local theater. Fanny, who had finished her lessons at the Royal Academy, accompanied him onstage.

But the romance offstage ended badly. George Beadnell, Maria's father, was a banker, and he found out about John Dickens's time in Marshalsea Prison. No debtor's son would have *his* daughter. He sent Maria off on a long trip. When she returned home, Maria called Charles "a boy" and sent him away.

Charles was devastated. He tried to mend the break, but the romance was over.

Trying not to think of Maria, Charles busied himself with writing. His work at Doctors' Commons paid the bills, but it seemed dull and uncreative. So Charles roamed the London streets, jotting down notes about the people and scenes he saw.

Early in 1832, Charles's uncle John Barrow came to him with a proposal. Barrow published a record of what was happening in Parliament—news about government leaders, bills being debated, laws that had been passed. The newspaper, called the

Mirror of Parliament, had room for another reporter, and Barrow wanted Charles to take on the job. (Charles's father already worked for the *Mirror.*) Charles joined the newspaper's staff.

The new reporter amazed those around him with his speedy note taking and his accuracy in changing these notes into articles. He won a place of honor among the ninety other men in the Parliamentary Press Gallery.

Within months of starting with the *Mirror,* Charles was approached about a second job. A new seven-penny paper called the *True Sun* was going to be published. Editor Samuel Blanchard needed a reporter who could write about everyday people and national occurrences. Charles took this job too.

Despite his hectic schedule, Charles continued his walks around London. To his observations, he would add his own creative style—a touch of humor, a speck of drama, and a few make-believe names. One of his finished pieces, "A Dinner at Poplar Walk," poked fun at a man with a spoiled son and a dog who tries to win the favor of his rich cousin—a middle-aged, prudish bachelor who hates children and pets.

On a November night in 1833, twenty-one-year-old Charles Dickens approached the outside letter box of a magazine office on Fleet Street. From under his cloak, he drew out his story about the cousins at Poplar Walk. His hand shook a little. Did he dare submit his manuscript to the popular *Monthly Magazine?*

Charles slipped the story into the letter slot and hurried away. Surely the piece would be rejected. But then again, maybe it wouldn't!

④

Boz is Born

Late on a December evening, Charles walked briskly into a bookstore on Strand Street.

May I have the latest *Monthly Magazine?* he asked, trying to hide the eagerness in his voice. He paid two shillings and a sixpence, and then walked a few paces away. He skimmed through the pages.

There it was—"A Dinner at Poplar Walk"—in all the glory of print. Charles hurried out of the bookstore, his eyes "so dimmed with pride and joy that they were not fit to be seen." Even if his name didn't appear with the article, it felt wonderful to be an author!

Within a few weeks, *Monthly Magazine* requested a few more humorous sketches from Mr. Charles Dickens. By August 1834, Charles was allowed to have his name appear with his articles. He decided to use a false name—that way if people didn't like the articles, no one would know he had written them. Charles had once nicknamed his youngest brother "Moses," but Augustus couldn't say the word. It had come out "Boses." Charles shortened it to Boz and made it his pen name.

How Londoners liked Boz! His characters seemed so real. "That Mrs. Leigh is just like our Auntie Belle," a London mother noted about one of Dickens's characters, "just one gossipy tale after another."

What began as a sprinkle of good fortune soon became a downpour. A new daily newspaper called the *Morning Chronicle* offered Charles a reporter's job. This proposal came at the right time, because Charles had quit his job at the *True Sun,* and he had work with the *Mirror* only when Parliament was in session. The *Morning Chronicle* would allow Charles to write his articles more creatively, so he accepted the paper's offer.

Dickens was soon sent to towns all over England to cover political speeches and important events. On the way home, by moonlight and by lantern, the dedicated reporter would write his articles as the carriage bounced over bumpy roads.

Charles had plenty of subjects on which to report. England was fast becoming known as the industrial center of the world. But the men, women, and children working in British factories were not being paid fairly or treated well. Factory workers, miners, and farmers were rioting for better conditions and the right to vote.

With the pay Charles earned from writing more creatively, he started dressing more creatively. He strode down the street in a new silk top hat and a handsome blue cloak lined with velvet.

John Dickens, however, was not faring as well as his son. The prison gates were opening for him once again, so Charles acted swiftly. He found his family less expensive living quarters and rented rooms for himself at the nearby Furnival's Inn. Living by himself, Charles wouldn't need to worry about keeping anyone awake when he wrote late into the night.

In 1835 the owners of the *Morning Chronicle* decided to publish an *Evening Chronicle* too. The new editor, George Hogarth, declared that articles by Boz had to be included, since "Everyone reads Boz!"

Dickens, though, wanted to write more than just an occasional article. He wanted a regular series of articles. Determined, Charles presented his case to Hogarth, and the editor agreed.

Charles Dickens will go far, thought Hogarth.

This young writer is charming, talented, and strong willed.

One night Hogarth invited Charles to his house for dinner to meet his wife and family. Catherine Hogarth, one of George's daughters, attracted Charles with her shy smile, large blue eyes, and long dark hair. Just nineteen, Catherine was as quiet as Maria had been flirtatious.

Charles returned to the Hogarth home many times that winter. His mischievous antics and clever mimicking would send Catherine and her younger sisters into long sessions of laughter.

After six months, Charles asked George for permission to marry Catherine. But family debts still hung over Dickens's head. So the engaged couple decided to wait to set the date.

Charles worked nearly day and night to earn enough money to marry his "dearest Kate." In addition to his other projects, Charles wrote two plays. And when the series of sketches for the *Evening Chronicle* was complete, Charles went right to work on a new series for another magazine. This time he called himself "Tibbs."

Dickens had caught the attention of the public and the publishing world. *Monthly Magazine* offered to publish some of Boz's sketches in a book. A deal was made, and the first edition of *Sketches by Boz* came out on Charles's birthday, February 7, 1836.

At twenty-four Charles Dickens had his first published book. Kate and Charles now felt confident about their future. They selected April 2, 1836, for their wedding day.

Before the flurry of preparations were far underway, a letter came from the *Library of Fiction* magazine. The editors wanted Charles to write a story to go along with a group of humorous illustrations by the popular artist Robert Seymour. The drawings were to be about a club of rough, uneducated sportsmen.

Charles liked the idea, but he had no intention of writing from illustrations. Seymour would draw from Charles's stories—not the other way around. Despite Seymour's angry protests, Charles got his way. The book would come out in monthly installments, with twenty episodes in twenty months.

Charles invented a character named Samuel Pickwick to lead the club of bumbling sportsmen in their trips around England. The first issue of *The Posthumous Papers of the Pickwick Club*, edited by Boz, arrived two days before Charles's wedding—a perfect gift for the young couple.

The wedding was small, with only the two families and a few guests attending. After the ceremony, Kate and Charles relaxed with a week's honeymoon in a village near Chatham. Then the newlyweds returned home to set up housekeeping at Furnival's Inn. Kate's sixteen-year-old sister, Mary, joined them to help out.

The household was soon running in a precisely ordered manner, and Charles returned to the tales of Samuel Pickwick. Unfortunately, readers were not as fond of *Pickwick* as they had been of his earlier works. Changes had to be made quickly.

A new illustrator, nicknamed "Phiz," took control of the art. And a new character, Sam Weller, captured readers with his clever cockney talk. "No noose is a good noose," Weller joked about the hanging rope. People liked his sayings so much that they began to use the witty remarks themselves. Sam's popular quips became known as "Wellerisms."

Sales leaped forward. By the last installment of *The Pickwick Papers*, in November 1836, sales had reached 40,000. "If I were to live a hundred years," Charles wrote, "and write three novels in each [year], I should never be so proud of any of them as I am of *Pickwick....*"

Success brought a round of new offers. Charles started working on a second series of *Sketches by Boz,* editing a new monthly story magazine called *Bentley's Miscellany,* and writing a story installment for each of the *Miscellany's* issues. Dickens now had enough income to quit newspaper reporting altogether. He could write stories full time, just as he wished. Charles's pen dashed across the pages (even turning out another play).

In January 1837, the first issue of *Bentley's Miscellany* appeared on newsstands. The new magazine contained the opening chapter of *The Adventures of Oliver Twist.*

By this time, most Londoners knew Boz's real identity. But readers discovered a different Charles Dickens in *Oliver Twist.* This story had a strong main character and a plot. Gone was Dickens's lighthearted humor—the cheerful comedy. In its place stood an orphan boy named Oliver, pitted against poverty and cruelty. *Oliver Twist* attacked English laws and the officials who failed to help Britain's children.

A few days after *Oliver Twist* came out, the Dickenses' first child was born—Charles Culliford Boz Dickens. Both the story and the baby received hearty welcomes. Charles was elated.

Despite the crowded conditions of the family's three rooms at Furnival's Inn, Charles noted in his diary, "I shall never be so happy again as in those chambers three storeys high—never if I roll in wealth and fame."

Still, those chambers proved to be too cramped for the growing family. When a twelve-room house at 48 Doughty Street became available at a reasonable price, Charles moved his family.

It was a grand feeling—having a new house, a new son, a successful career, and a caring family. But Charles did not have long to enjoy it all.

One evening in May, Kate's sister Mary collapsed of a heart attack after an evening at the theater. By the next afternoon, she was dead.

Charles was so overwhelmed by grief he could not work. Many months passed before Charles was able to return to his deadlines. But even then he felt disheartened.

To research his next story, Charles visited several boarding schools under a false name. He told principals that he was searching for the right school for a friend's son. But he was really checking out how children were being treated in these places. When readers picked up the completed novel, *Nicholas Nickleby*, they were shocked by Dickens's descriptions of the conditions in some English boarding schools.

As the new year came, Charles and Kate were looking forward to the birth of another child. On March 6, 1838, their first daughter was born. The proud parents named her Mary.

In four short years, Charles's writing had brought him fame and fortune. But he still longed to break into the upper circles of English society. He worked harder than ever. In June of 1838, the prestigious Athenaeum Club asked Charles to become a member. As far as Charles was concerned, only the finest, most literary people in England belonged to this group. Now *he* was one of them.

If the Dickens family were truly to enter the ranks of the upper classes, however, another step seemed in order—a move to a better neighborhood. Charles chose a fancy three-story house in the Regent's Park area of London.

The installments of *Pickwick* and *Oliver Twist* were now published in book form, and money poured in. But Charles had problems with his publishers. He would fight stubbornly for money and control, as well as to get out of contracts he no longer liked.

Charles quit working for *Bentley's Miscellany*.

He had grown tired of writing stories for other people's magazines. So he made a deal with his publishers to start his own weekly journal—*Master Humphrey's Clock.* The first issue came out on April 4, 1840. It featured a description of an old curiosity-shop owner who kept odd manuscripts inside an old clock. The manuscripts were the magazine's stories.

Sales were brisk for the first few issues, but then they dropped off. Charles's readers wanted an on-going story. Dickens responded by introducing the owner's grandchild, Little Nell, into the magazine and forming a story around her.

As months went by, the child grew seriously ill, and readers wrote to Charles begging him to spare her. But Charles couldn't. Remembering his sister-in-law Mary, Charles started working on Nell's death scene. The tears flowed as he wrote. Later his readers wept too. The completed story, *The Old Curiosity Shop*, found a favored place with Dickens's fans.

Without Nell, though, Charles feared his readers would lose interest in his magazine. Only a new story and character would hold their attention. Thus he began *Barnaby Rudge*, and another novel joined the growing Dickens collection.

Over the years, the number of Dickens children had also grown steadily. Charles ran his household with loving but strict military order. Even so, the noise and distractions kept increasing. Charles often had to retreat to his writing chambers to concentrate.

All the while, Dickens's loyal readers kept clamoring for more stories. Requests even began to come from across the Atlantic Ocean. American publishers had pirated Dickens's works, selling his stories in the United States without paying for them. There were no American copyright laws to protect works by British authors or British laws to protect works by American authors.

When Dickens realized that his stories had been stolen, he lost his temper. Yet he was flattered that Americans liked his stories.

Maybe it's time, he thought, that I meet these Americans myself.

⑤
Off to America

As the year 1842 approached, Charles became thoroughly excited about his plans to visit the United States. "I cannot describe to you the glow into which I rise," he wrote the editor of a popular American magazine.

Charles wanted a rest from his exhausting weekly deadlines. But he hated to say farewell to his readers in England. He would miss them. In the final issue of *Master Humphrey's Clock*, in November 1841, Charles addressed his readers directly. He wrote that he regretted his American trip would keep him from them for so long a time.

The trip's length bothered Kate as well. It would take several months, she argued, and she did not want to leave the children for that long. But Charles stood firm. He was confident his brother Fred and some family friends could manage the children while they were gone. Besides, he reasoned, Georgina, Kate's fifteen-year-old sister, had volunteered to care of the children. Crying a bit, Kate finally gave in, agreeing to her husband's commands.

On January 4, 1842, Charles and Kate sailed from England aboard the steamship *Britannia.* After eighteen days filled with storms and seasickness, the ship docked in Boston.

Never did Charles or Kate expect such a grand greeting. To his friend John Forster, Charles wrote, "How can I give you the faintest notion of my reception here; of the crowds that pour in and out the whole day; of the . . . welcomes of all kinds, balls, dinners, assemblies without end?"

Charles cut an impressive figure as he stood in front of the American crowds. Under a shaggy greatcoat of buffalo skin, he wore a decorative red waistcoat, a gold watch-chain, and a many-folded scarf. Always an actor, Charles now had America for his stage.

Some of the country's finest writers greeted the British visitors and engaged Charles in lively debates. Interested in the workings of a democracy, Charles also made it a point to talk to lawmakers and elected officials. He visited President John Tyler in the White House and former President John Quincy Adams in his home.

As the Dickenses traveled around the United States, from Boston, Massachusetts, to St. Louis, Missouri, Charles insisted on seeing sights beyond the fine hotels and grand ballrooms. He visited the slums, the prisons, and the factories. He walked around plantations worked by slaves. Slavery made Charles sick with anger. America was not the ideal place he had dreamed it would be.

After six months, Charles was weary of his role as a distinguished visitor. The constant parties and the countless hands to shake had become chores. He couldn't tolerate the American habit of tobacco chewing and spitting. And when Charles spoke out against the lack of copyright protection for British works in America, reporters attacked him. Angry and tired, Charles called an end to the performance, and the Dickenses headed home.

That fall, in 1842, readers scrambled to buy Dickens's *American Notes*. Most British fans chuckled over Charles's comments, both positive and negative. But readers in the United States did not like his criticisms. They felt that it was "unfitting and improper" for Dickens to criticize his hosts.

Almost immediately, Charles began a new novel, *The Life and Adventures of Martin Chuzzlewit*.

The first few installments, however, did not sell well. And Charles needed money. Not only did he have his expanding household to pay for, but he was also supporting his brothers, and he had to pull his father out of debt once more.

Charles quickly put together a short story about how greed can destroy a person. He used a heartless character named Ebenezer Scrooge to show how an "economic man" can lose himself to money. Only the visits of three Christmas spirits could save the miserly Scrooge. In the end, goodness triumphs!

Through *A Christmas Carol in Prose: A Ghost Story of Christmas,* Charles won his readers back. Yet he failed to make the money he had hoped for.

Back to the writing desk he went. But Charles had a difficult time working. He needed a change, so he packed up the family and servants for a trip to Italy. Kate's sister Georgina, who was now known as Aunt Georgy, came as well. She had become a permanent part of the Dickens household.

Charles hoped to find fresh ideas in Italy. Instead, he found it more difficult to write away from the familiar streets of London. The Italian summer heat made his legs swell, and the clanging of church bells at all hours nearly drove him mad.

By September of 1844, Charles Dickens felt old, worn out, and unable to write.

Then inspiration struck. The church chimes whisked his thoughts back to London—to a poor porter named Trotty Veck, standing before a church and hearing its bells. A month later, the story was done. Charles hurried back to England to give it to his publishers.

As soon as *The Chimes* appeared, an eager public gobbled it up. Readers knew at once that the chimes rang out a cry for justice—for jobs and for fair laws.

Charles no longer feared he had lost his talent. At the age of thirty-three, his energy seemed limitless. He promised his publishers another Christmas story for the next year, which became *The Cricket on the Hearth*. He also started editing his notes on his Italian trip. These were eventually bound in a volume called *Pictures from Italy*.

Then Charles announced his latest plan—to start a newspaper. He wanted his paper, the *Daily News*, to make people aware of injustices. The first issue reached readers on January 21, 1846.

The paper won little attention, so Charles ordered his reporters to do more than just report.

They had to start asking questions: Why did that fire happen? How could it have been prevented?

Unfortunately, Charles's work on the *Daily News* took him away from his story writing, which he missed. After seventeen days as editor, Dickens persuaded his friend John Forster to take over. Then Charles started plotting out another series—*Dombey and Son*—and a Christmas tale for 1846—*The Battle of Life*.

Charles drove himself to exhaustion to make his deadlines. He would write until he had the exact number of words required to fill the pages he had promised his publishers.

Still, Charles would take breaks from his writing to pursue his other great interest—acting. Occasionally he would even coax Kate and some of the children to join him onstage. Across the British Isles, crowds would swarm into playhouses to see the Dickens family performing with their traveling theater troupe.

As 1846 passed into 1847, Charles had to struggle more and more with his writing. *Dombey and Son* came slowly, and the thought of writing another Christmas story didn't appeal to Charles. He was more interested in acting, traveling, and working for charitable causes.

No Christmas story was written for 1847. *The Haunted Man,* Dickens's last Christmas book by himself, came out late in 1848.

In 1849 Charles Dickens was proclaimed the best-known man in all of England, according to a poll taken by the *London Times.* Ranked with Queen Victoria, Charles had fans around the world.

Dickens's family had increased almost as quickly as his fame. At thirty-seven Charles Dickens was the father of six sons and two daughters—not to mention countless characters on paper.

No one could say that Charles Dickens was not productive. And he wasn't finished yet!

6

World of Shadows

By the mid-1800s, Charles had started to notice struggles within himself. A distance had begun to grow between himself and Kate. They argued more frequently. He would snap at Kate because her slower, quieter ways annoyed him. And Kate would complain about the attention Charles paid his female fans. Though he was surrounded by friends and family, Charles felt lonely. He longed for something better.

Throughout England and much of the world, Charles Dickens's words carried force and power. Thanks in part to him, Parliament was making new laws to protect and aid England's poor. But the numbers of the hungry and the weary continued to grow. And this depressed Dickens.

Filled with raging emotions, Charles began a new novel. He created a character, David Copperfield, who would tell his own life's story. But it was more than David's life; it was Dickens's life too. Many of the story's characters resembled people Dickens had known. Mr. and Mrs. Micawber, the people young David lived with, were like Charles's parents; while David's love for Dora, was similar to Charles's love for Maria Beadnell. And the grief David felt at Dora's death was just as intense as the anguish Charles felt at the death of Kate's sister Mary.

Sometimes Charles had trouble keeping his real life and his creative life separate. It was not surprising that when a daughter was born to the Dickenses in August 1850, Charles named her Dora.

By October *David Copperfield* was finished. Charles found it difficult to put the project away. He wrote to his friend, "Oh my dear Forster, if I were to say half of what Copperfield made me feel tonight, I should be turned inside out! I seem to be sending some part of myself into a shadowy world."

That shadowy world, though, greeted *David Copperfield* with great acclaim. Many agreed that this latest effort was Dickens's best.

Charles wasted little time congratulating himself. He threw his energy into starting a new monthly magazine for entertainment and enlightenment called *Household Words.*

Then during a two-week period in 1851, Charles's father and his beloved baby Dora both died. Though grieving himself, Charles took time out to help Kate and his family adjust.

That summer Charles decided a change was in order. The Dickenses would move to a new address in London—a prestigious place called Tavistock House. On top of the move, Charles started a new story series—*Bleak House.* The story's first installment in *Household Words* caused a greater stir than even *Copperfield* had.

Dickens had reached the top. At the age of forty, Charles was expecting the birth of his tenth child and the publication of his sixteenth book.

Not yet content, Charles began another novel that described how he felt as a child—*Hard Times.* It exposed the sad lives of children working in English factories. Soon after the book's first few installments appeared, a debate over child-labor laws raged in Parliament.

Charles did not let up. On the heels of *Hard Times* came *Little Dorrit,* a novel that attacked debtors' prisons. Parliament was pushed to debate these laws as well.

Writing novels, however, no longer satisfied Charles. Audiences filled theaters to hear the noted author read and act out his works. Laughing, shouting, weeping, Charles kept his fans entranced.

Charles had come a long way from the boy he had been in Chatham. But one day in 1857, Charles took a walk with a friend around his childhood haunts. Outside of Rochester, the two stopped to admire the red-brick house on top of Gad's Hill.

"Long ago," Charles told his friend, "my father told me that I might come to live in that house if I became a successful man. It's a dream I've always had."

Charles's friend checked with the owner and found that Gad's Hill was for sale. Within weeks Charles's dream had become real. He bought Gad's Hill Place and arranged to live there during summers.

As one dream blossomed, though, another wilted. Charles and Kate were now spending more and more time apart. Finally in 1858, Kate returned to the Hogarth family home for good, and Charles kept the children with him. But he sent his eldest son, Charles, Jr., to his mother to care for her.

Georgina remained with the Dickens family to help look after the children.

The shadows of Charles's personal life entered his professional life too. He was forced to defend himself against the scandal of his separation from Kate. He argued frequently with his publishers and his friends—even Forster. In 1859 Charles discontinued *Household Words* in an angry huff.

Within days Charles started a new weekly magazine—*All Year Round*. In the first issue, Dickens's new novel, *A Tale of Two Cities*, swept readers into the French Revolution.

Charles was nearing fifty years old. He noted with sadness the loss of many of his friends and family. He wrote, "It's an emptier world each day."

To fight the loneliness, Charles sometimes spent time with a young actress named Ellen Ternan. But this did not keep away his feelings of depression. Charles was an idealist, and his childhood, his marriage, and his country had not lived up to what he thought they should be. Even his children, though they delighted him, gave him great disappointments. He often disapproved of their choices, and he would vigorously tell them so.

As the children grew older, Dickens sold Tavistock so he could live year-round at Gad's Hill. He had a comfortable writing studio there. Hans Christian Andersen, a famous Danish writer, had sent Dickens a small Swiss chalet to thank Charles for a long British visit. Dickens had a tunnel built from the house to the chalet so he could use the chalet for his writing chambers—no matter the season.

Summers brought many visitors to Gad's Hill. Charles's daughters Mary and Kate were often at his side. Although no one saw Charles without a crisp waistcoat and tie, some guests whispered that his beard and mustache grew shaggier with each passing year.

But Charles never ceased to surprise them. With his strong sense of humor and flair for the dramatic, he kept his friends guessing. On several occasions, Charles started one of his home readings by coming in through the window.

Invitations for readings continued to pour in. Despite his children's pleas for him to rest, Charles accepted the offers. He also worked many hours on a novel about an orphan named Pip who wanted to become rich and educated. Readers waited anxiously for each installment of *Great Expectations.*

The older Charles grew, the more his mind turned to thoughts of mystery and death. In his next novel, *Our Mutual Friend,* Charles described a murder.

He used the crime to point an accusing finger at the English education system.

When the United States's Civil War was over, Charles accepted invitations to return to America. Once there he was treated to a whirl of parties and receptions. This time there were no criticisms. Charles wrote, "the people here know how to treat a guest."

Charles's pace slowed once he returned to England. He walked unsteadily at times, bothered again by swelling in his legs. He could now write for only a few hours a day. This time he worked on a dark tale about a drug addict. But *The Mystery of Edwin Drood* would never be finished.

On the morning of June 9, 1870, Charles Dickens died of a stroke. He was fifty-eight years old. News of his death stunned people around the world. *The London Times* reported that his death day "...will be an evil day in the memories of all who can appreciate true genius and admire its matchless works."

Poet Henry Wadsworth Longfellow wrote to John Forster from the United States, "I never knew an author's death to cause such general mourning. It is no exaggeration to say that the whole country is stricken with grief."

Charles had requested a simple burial. He had ordered that his funeral be private and that anyone attending "wear no scarf, cloak, black bow, long hat band, or other such revolting absurdity." His tombstone, he had insisted, should bear only his name, without an added Mr. or Esquire. A burial plot outside Rochester would suit him fine.

It was not to be, however, not for the man who had changed lives and laws through his words. After thousands came to mourn him, Charles Dickens was laid to rest in London's grand Westminister Abbey—a place reserved for the famous and the great.

Book List

For further reading, try a book by Charles Dickens:

Sketches by Boz 1833-1836
The Pickwick Papers 1836-1837
Oliver Twist 1837-1838
Nicholas Nickleby 1838-1839
The Old Curiosity Shop 1840-1841
Barnaby Rudge 1841
American Notes 1842
Martin Chuzzlewit 1843-1844
A Christmas Carol 1843
The Chimes 1844
The Cricket on the Hearth 1845
Pictures from Italy 1846
Dombey and Son 1846-1848
The Battle of Life 1846
The Haunted Man 1848
David Copperfield 1849-1850
Bleak House 1852-1853
Hard Times 1854
Little Dorrit 1855-1857
A Tale of Two Cities 1859
Great Expectations 1860-1861
Our Mutual Friend 1864-1865
The Mystery of Edwin Drood
  (begun but never finished) 1869-1870

Bibliography

Allen, Michael. *Charles Dickens' Childhood.* New York: St. Martin's Press, 1988.

Dexter, Walter, ed. *Mr. and Mrs. Charles Dickens: His Letters to Her.* New York: Haskell House Publishers, 1972.

Fido, Martin. *Charles Dickens.* London: The Hamlyn Publishing Group, 1968.

Johnson, Edgar. *Charles Dickens — His Tragedy and Triumph.* New York: Simon and Schuster, 1977.

MacKenzie, Norman and Jeanne. *Dickens — A Life.* New York: Oxford University Press, 1979.

Mankowitz, Wolf. *Dickens of London.* New York: Macmillan Publishing, 1976.

Priestley, J. B. *Charles Dickens: A Pictorial Biography.* New York: Viking, 1962.

Wagenkneckt, Edward. *An Introduction to Charles Dickens.* Chicago: Scott Foresman and Co., 1952.

Wilson, Angus. *The World of Charles Dickens.* New York: Viking, 1970.